Learn to Draw

Disney

Celebrated Characters Collection

Walter Foster
Jr.

Published by Walter Foster Jr.,
an imprint of The Quarto Group
26391 Crown Valley Parkway, Suite 220, Mission Viejo, CA 92691
www.QuartoKnows.com

Printed in China
3 5 7 9 10 8 6 4 2

Learn to Draw Disney

Celebrated Characters Collection

Table of Contents

Tools & Materials

Before you begin, you will need to gather a few simple tools. Start with a regular pencil so you can easily erase any mistakes. Make sure to have an eraser and pencil sharpener too! When you're finished with your drawing, you can bring your characters to life by adding color. Just grab some colored pencils, markers, or even watercolor or acrylic paints.

eraser

drawing pencil and paper

sharpener

colored pencils

felt-tip markers

paintbrush and paints

How to Use This Book

Artists draw characters in several steps. They start with basic shapes and add more details with each step. In this book, the blue lines show each new step. The black lines show what you've already drawn.

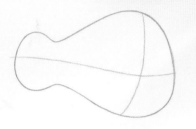

STEP 1

First draw the basic shapes.

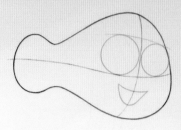

STEP 2

Each new step is shown in blue.

STEP 3

Follow the blue lines to add the details.

STEP 4

Now darken the lines you want to keep and erase the rest.

STEP 5

Add color!

Drawing Exercises

Warm up your hand by drawing squiggles
and shapes on a piece of scrap paper.

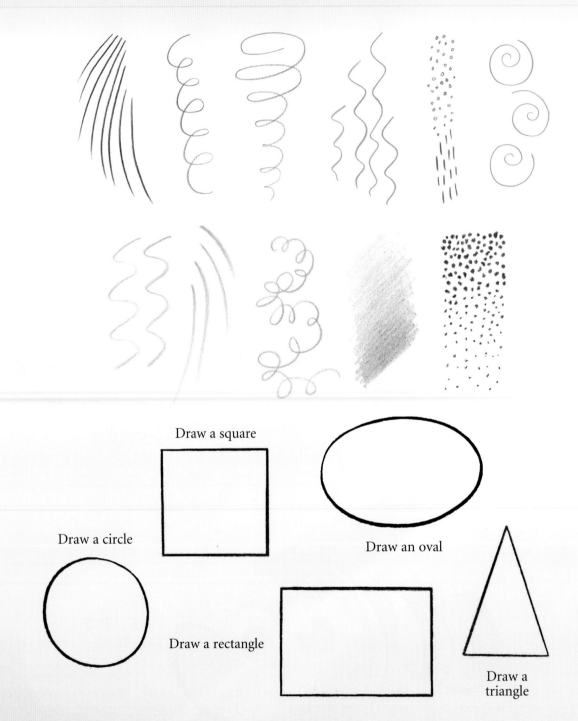

Draw a square

Draw a circle

Draw an oval

Draw a rectangle

Draw a
triangle

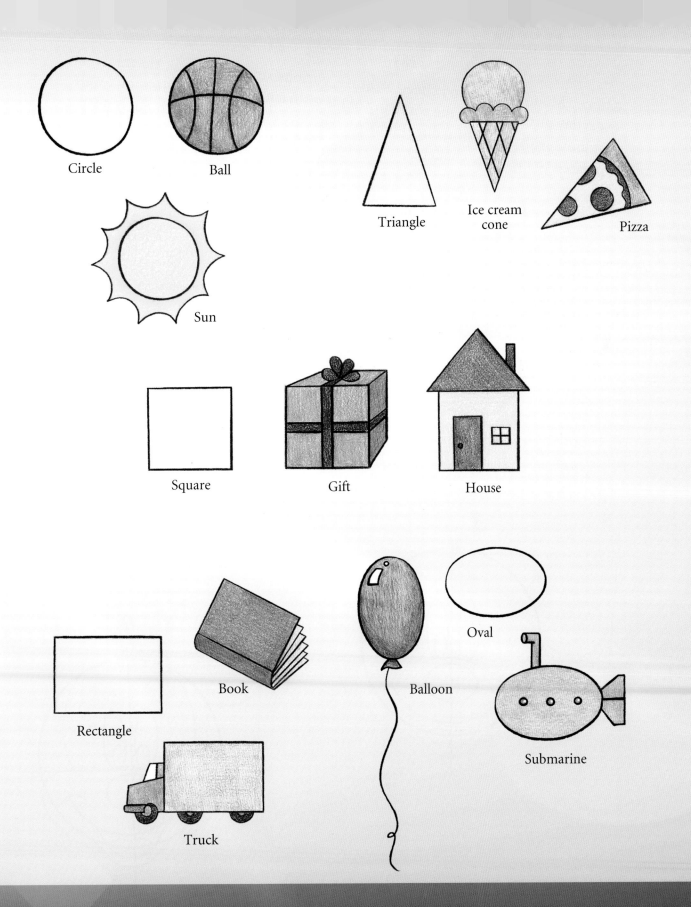

Circle

Ball

Triangle

Ice cream cone

Pizza

Sun

Square

Gift

House

Rectangle

Book

Balloon

Oval

Submarine

Truck

MICKEY MOUSE

Mickey Mouse is kind and cheerful, brave, curious, and a great pal. He enjoys everyday pleasures, like the company of his girlfriend, Minnie, friends, or a walk outdoors with his faithful dog, Pluto. Mickey loves laughter and fun but is also prepared to meet any challenge that comes his way!

1

2

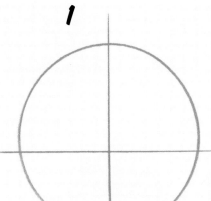

3

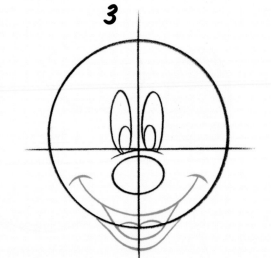

4

5

6

MICKEY MOUSE

1

WHEN MICKEY IS
SURPRISED, HIS EARS
GO UP

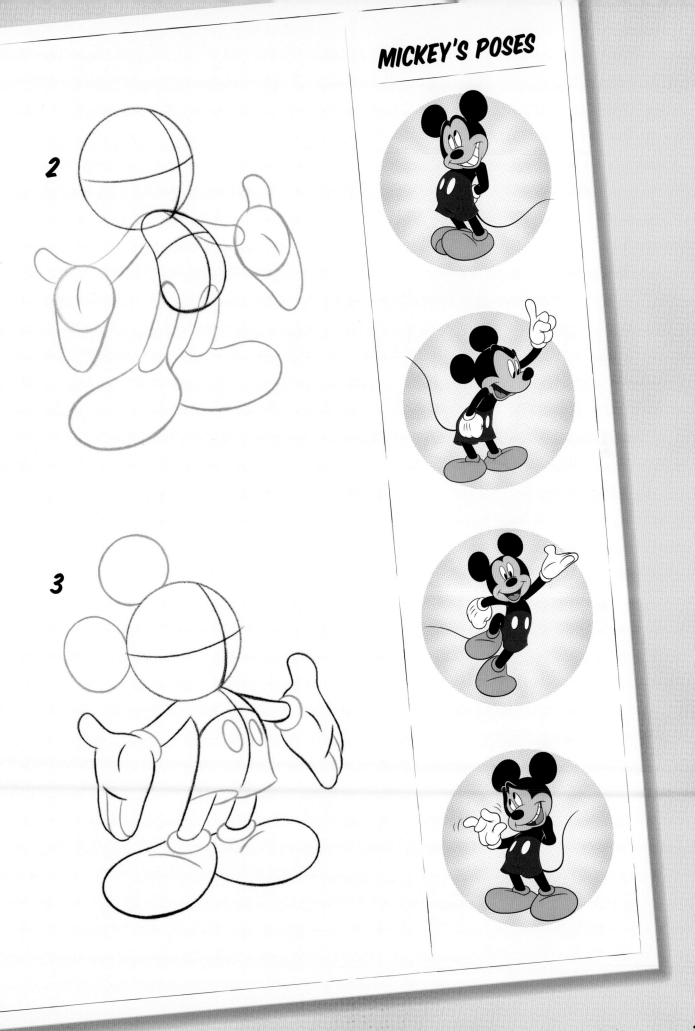

2

3

4

MICKEY'S EYEBROWS CAN
SHOW HOW HE'S FEELING

5

YOU CAN ALWAYS SEE BOTH OF MICKEY'S
EARS, NO MATTER WHICH DIRECTION HIS
HEAD IS TURNED

WHEN THE TOPS OF MICKEY'S HANDS SHOW, BE SURE TO ADD THE STITCHING LINES TO HIS GLOVES

6

MICKEY'S POSES

MICKEY'S SHOES ARE SLIGHTLY LONGER THAN HIS HANDS

MINNIE MOUSE

Minnie is a free-spirited, active mouse with intelligence and endless interests, including reading, traveling, dancing, and listening to music. Minnie plunges herself into all kinds of adventures, especially the fun kind, but she's savvy and knows to stay away from danger and bad decisions. She has a special bond with animals, nature, and, of course, her boyfriend, Mickey, and the rest of her friends!

1

2

3

4

5

6

MINNIE MOUSE

1

MINNIE'S BOW IS LARGE AND FULL IN
FORM. IT BENDS BACK SLIGHTLY IN
PROFILE OR REAR VIEWS

2

3

4

MINNIE'S SHOES HAVE A WIDE,
POINTED TOE AND THICK, HIGH HEELS

5

YOU CAN CHANGE MINNIE'S
EXPRESSION BY TILTING HER HEAD

MINNIE'S HEAD IS SIMILAR TO MICKEY'S, BUT MINNIE'S EYES ARE SLIGHTLY LARGER AND WIDER, AND HER OPEN MOUTH IS SLIGHTLY SMALLER

6

MINNIE'S POSES

PLUTO

Pluto is full grown but has the spirit of a puppy. He is friendly, happy, and always ready to play, but he can become a tough guard dog when necessary. A loyal companion, he is always there for Mickey, his owner.

1

2

HIS COLLAR HANGS LOOSELY AT THE BACK OF HIS NECK

PLUTO'S EARS CAN ACT
TOGETHER TO ACCENTUATE
A MOOD OR AN EXPRESSION

3

4

5

GOOFY

Goofy has a sensitive soul and becomes very attached to things—such as his now-ancient car—and he would rather store everything in his chaotic attic than throw it away. There's nothing Goofy wouldn't do for his friends—especially his best friend, Mickey.

4

NOTICE HOW THE WHITES OF
GOOFY'S EYES TOUCH EACH
OTHER; JUST MAKE SURE YOU
KEEP HIS PUPILS SEPARATE

GOOFY'S HEAD IS SIMILAR
TO PLUTO'S

5

6

DONALD DUCK

Donald Duck has quite a temper, but despite his ways, it's hard not to like him. He goes on all sorts of adventures, certain that he'll be successful in whatever he tries. But because he always takes the quickest and easiest route, he ends up on the path to total disaster!

1

2

3

DONALD'S HANDS ARE ALMOST
AS LONG AS THE HEIGHT
OF HIS HEAD

4

5

DONALD'S FACE CHANGES WHEN HE'S IN DIFFERENT MOODS

6

DONALD'S HAT IS SOFT AND FLEXIBLE, BUT IT ALWAYS HOLDS ITS SHAPE

Winnie the Pooh

Pooh is a bear of little brain and big tummy. He has a one-food mind when it comes to honey. He is also a good friend to Piglet and a perfect pal for "doing nothing" with Christopher Robin. Pooh has a simple sweetness to him that goes beyond the honey stuck to his paws.

1

2

Pooh's ears are halfway between the top and back of his head

his eyes are set on the muzzle line

3

4

the length of Pooh's arms ends at the widest part of his tummy

7

Pooh's hands are simple—no fingers, just thumbs

8

Tigger

Tigger is one of a kind in the Hundred-Acre Wood. He is always sure of "what tiggers do best," even before he does something. But perhaps the really "wonderful thing" about Tigger is the bounce he brings to everyone around him.

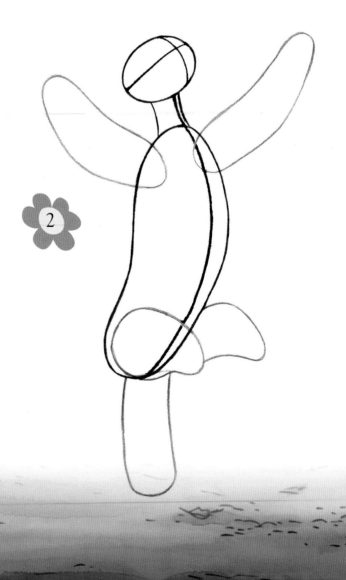

3

4

Tigger's tail is
like a spring when
he bounces

When Tigger is standing or walking, his tail is angular, as if a spring is coiled inside

Tigger's hands are like
mittens with no fingers

Piglet

It's not easy being a very small animal in a very big wood. Piglet is little enough to be swept away by a leaf and timid enough to be scared by his friends' monster stories. Despite his small size, Piglet has a really big heart! Piglet is one of Pooh's closest friends in the Hundred-Acre Wood.

Piglet's ears attach to the side of his head

4

5

Piglet's clothing lines should wrap around his body

YES!

round

NO!

flat

6

Eeyore

Things are always looking down for Eeyore. With a tail that comes loose and a house that collapses, he's always ready for things to go wrong. Still, Eeyore manages to smile once in a while, even though he's almost always gloomy.

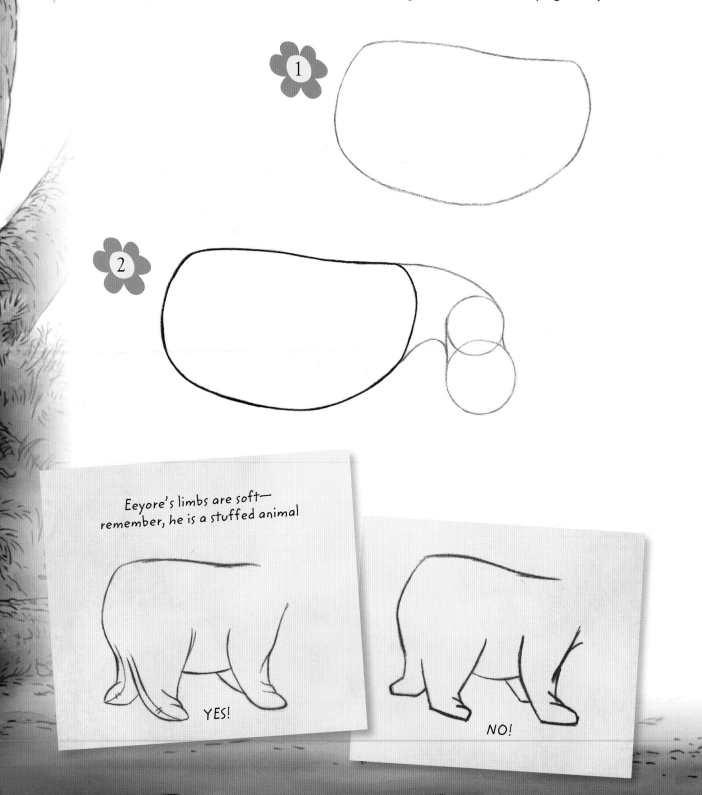

1

2

Eeyore's limbs are soft—remember, he is a stuffed animal

YES!

NO!

his neck and head are just
about the same length

Eeyore's face starts with
2 circles—a small one for
the head and a larger one
for the muzzle

8

SIMBA

Simba can't wait to be king. But when a wildebeest stampede kills his father, King Mufasa, his evil uncle Scar blames Simba and convinces him to run away. Simba befriends Timon and Pumbaa and lives a carefree lifestyle of hakuna matata. But one day, after his old friend Nala appears and pleads with him to save the Pride Lands from Scar, Simba springs into action to take his rightful place as the Lion King.

6

7

MUFASA

Mufasa is a stern but kind leader. He is a caring and nurturing father and adoring husband. He is courageous, yet cautious, and is respected by everyone except for his brother, Scar. Mufasa's jealous brother is a thorn in the king's side, but Mufasa still looks out for him, hoping that someday he will change.

SCAR

Scar, the evil brother of Mufasa, wants to be king. He is witty, seductive, and willing to do anything to gain power—even if it means killing his brother and blaming his nephew Simba. Scar becomes king of the Pride Lands, but his rule devastates the land and endangers the pride.

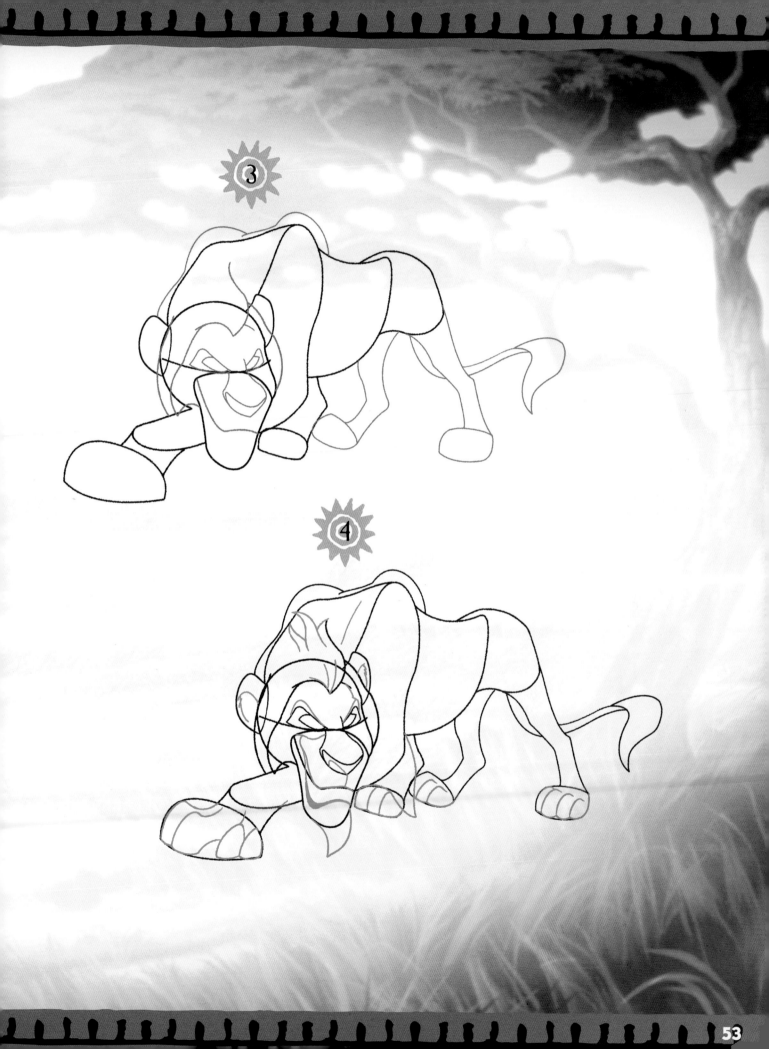

5

6

TOY STORY

WOODY

Woody is a cowboy sheriff doll with a pull-string that, when pulled, proclaims Woody's signature catchphrases from the 1950s TV show *Woody's Roundup*. He's always been Andy's favorite toy. Woody is the toys' dependable leader, and he ensures that no toy ever gets left behind.

sheriff badge is a 5-point star

STEP 1

STEP 2

Woody is about 4 heads tall

top view of
Woody's hat

there is
stitching
around the
edges

hat band comes up 1/4
of hat height

buckle has a
steer-head
design

8-pointed
spurs

STEP
3

STEP
4

Buzz Lightyear

Buzz Lightyear is a heroic space ranger action figure, complete with laser beam, karate-chop action, and pop-out wings. Buzz is a kid's dream toy who quickly becomes a favorite of young Andy, and the closest of buddies with Woody.

STEP 1

STEP 2

STEP 3

iris is about ⅓ the size of the eye

YES!   NO!

brow should barely touch eye in normal pose; keep brows thick

the chin cleft is ½ the distance between lower lip and chin

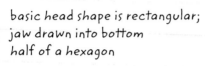
basic head shape is rectangular; jaw drawn into bottom half of a hexagon

Buzz's chin takes up about $\frac{1}{3}$ of his head

chin cleft looks like the number 9

eyes can change shape in exaggerated expressions

SPACE RANGER LIGHTYEAR

Jessie

Jessie knows what it means to be a toy. She once belonged to a little girl who loved her as much as Andy loves Woody. But when that little girl gave Jessie away, the brokenhearted cowgirl decided that being a collectible is better than being with a child who might outgrow you. Woody has to remind Jessie what being a toy is all about.

STEP 1

YES! she has a button nose

NO!

3 fringe pieces

stitching wraps around cuff

shirt and gauntlet pattern

don't forget
her ponytail

Woody's hat is
triangular

Jessie's hat is
rounder

STEP 2

her hat usually
sits on the back
of her head

STEP 3

Jessie's body is
flexible like a
rag doll's

STEP 4

LOTSO

Lots-o'-Huggin' Bear, or "Lotso" as he likes to be called, is a strawberry-scented, plush pink teddy bear with a kind smile and a pudgy belly. He's the boss at Sunnyside Daycare, and his easygoing, homespun manner puts newly donated toys at ease. But there's a dark side to Lotso; he runs a tight ship and won't tolerate any toys that question his authority.

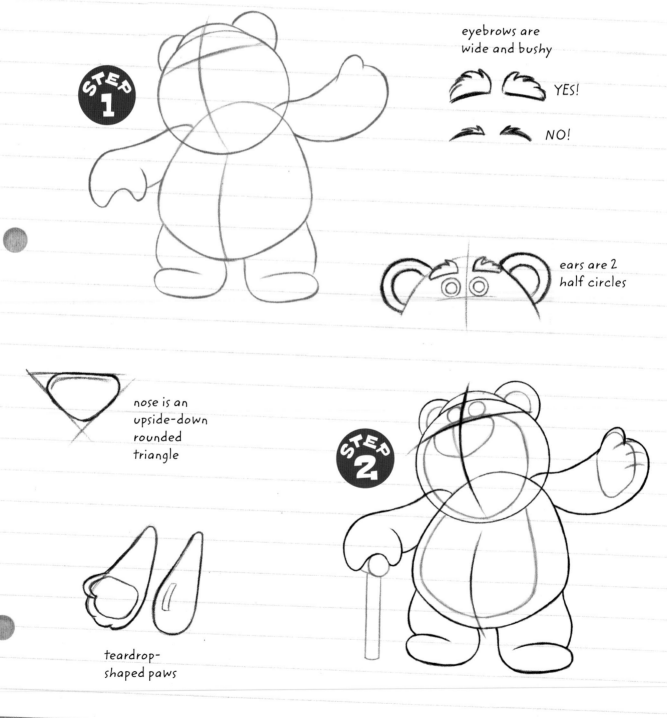

STEP 1

eyebrows are wide and bushy

YES!

NO!

ears are 2 half circles

nose is an upside-down rounded triangle

STEP 2

teardrop-shaped paws

STEP 3

I'M A HUGGER

eyes are round and set close together

STEP 4

his cane is a wooden mallet

Nemo

Nemo is a curious and impressionable young clownfish who lives with his overprotective, single-parent father, Marlin. Despite being born with a withered fin, Nemo yearns for adventure, and as fate takes him far from home, he learns he is capable of doing great things.

1

from the side, Nemo is shaped like a Goldfish® cracker

from the front, his body looks like a gumdrop

2

3

YES! top (dorsal) fin is 2 different shapes pointing at different angles

NO! too even; too upright

4

top fin is same
height as one eye

Nemo is about
4 "eyes" tall,
including top fin

4
3
2
1
0

YES! bottom fins are set
apart from each other

NO! fins look
like bow tie

7

Dory

Throughout the vast ocean you will not find a fish more hospitable, more friendly, and more sociable than Dory. She would love to chat with you all day and tell you her life story...but she can't. Dory suffers from short-term memory loss. But to Dory, the glass is always half-full.

1

2

3

from the side, Dory's body is shaped like a football

Dory is just over 4 times the length of Nemo

4

side fins are
straight on top

3 rays

and curved
on bottom

from the front, Dory's stripe defines where her "eyebrows" end

freckles follow the curved bridge of her "nose"

YES! curved freckle pattern

NO! too straight

7

Marlin

After losing his wife and family to the ocean, Marlin is left alone to raise his only surviving child, Nemo. He struggles with his inability to let go as his son becomes more independent and begins school. When Nemo is suddenly taken away by scuba divers, Marlin must find the courage to venture beyond the shelter of the reef so he can bring his boy home.

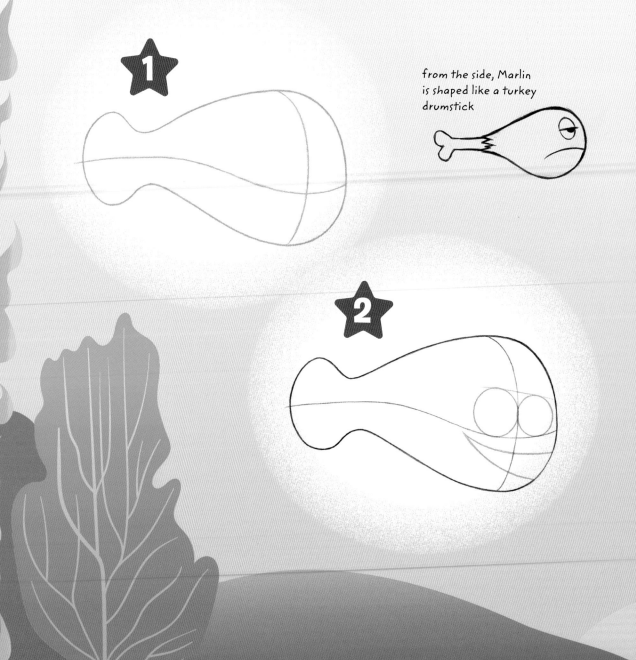

from the side, Marlin is shaped like a turkey drumstick

3

Marlin is about 2 times
the size of Nemo

4

Marlin's face is kind of flat

5 rays on side (pectoral) fins and tail

7

YES!
eyes close
together

NO! eyes
too far apart

bags under
his eyes make
him look tired

MR. INCREDIBLE

A man of super strength, Mr. Incredible was once the best-known, most popular Super alive! Then, through the Super Relocation Program, Mr. Incredible became "normal" Bob Parr, a claims adjuster at probably the worst insurance company ever. But Bob is not content with his ordinary life. He misses being a Super. One day, a mysterious summons calls the hero back to action...

Bob has a very large chin and an arched nose

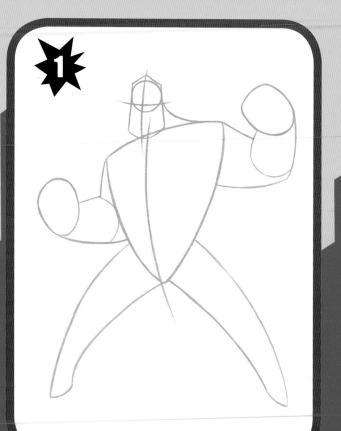

3

4

5

head shape

YES!
rounded bottom

NO!
not straight

ELASTIGIRL

Helen Parr, formerly a Super named Elastigirl, has adjusted to normal life quite well and is busily focused on caring for her three children. While she occasionally uses her amazing ability to stretch, she is careful to do so only behind closed doors. She misses the old days but doesn't dwell on those times. She only wishes Bob would do—and feel—the same.

1

2

keep
bridge of
nose short

YES!
short

NO!
not long

3

body shape is almost like a figure 8

4

5

Violet

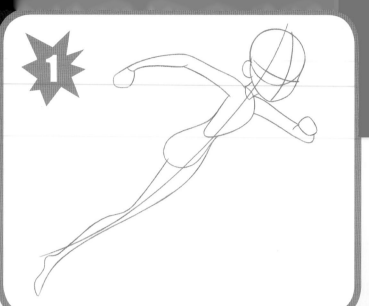

Violet Parr is, in many ways, a typical shy, insecure teenage girl. She, like her parents, has special powers, and it seems only right that hers allow her to turn invisible and protect herself with an impenetrable force field. For what would be better for an awkward young woman than to be invisible at a moment's notice? This is especially true for Violet—someone who desperately wants to be normal, but truly isn't.

DASH

At age 10, Dash seems to be moving even when standing still. He is always full of restless energy due mostly to his power of Super speed. Unable to resist torturing his least favorite teacher, Dash has been called into the principal's office more than once, but he's never been caught. Dash doesn't understand why Supers should hide their powers. Why would they have them if they weren't supposed to use them?

1

2

JACK-JACK

Jack-Jack's family thinks he is the only normal one among them. He acts just like any kid who is nearly 2 years old: He jabbers in gibberish and spits out half the food spooned into his mouth. But one day he surprises everyone when he turns into a ball of fire and eventually a raging, monster-like little muscle man.

1

FROZONE

Frozone was once known as the coolest Super on the planet. With the ability to create ice from the moisture in the air, he can build ice bridges, skate across them with special boots, and freeze criminals right in their tracks. Known as Lucius Best in his secret life, Frozone is also Mr. Incredible's best friend—and a reluctant partner in Bob's undercover heroics.

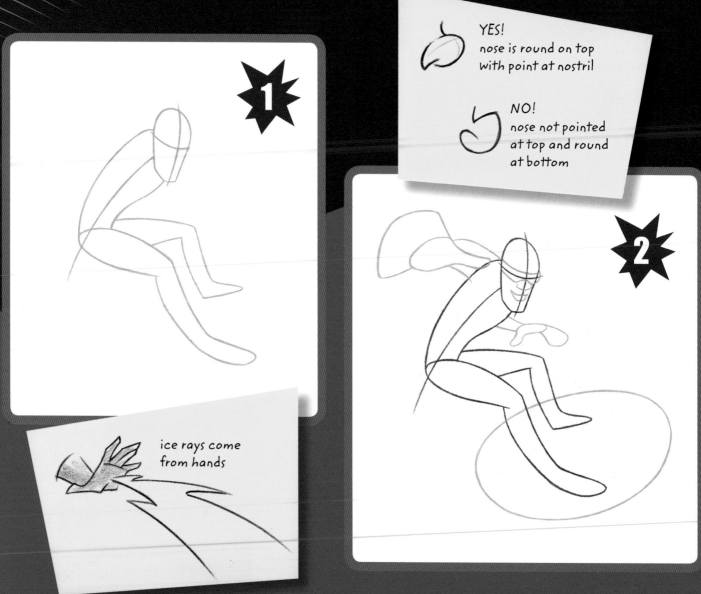

YES!
nose is round on top
with point at nostril

NO!
nose not pointed
at top and round
at bottom

ice rays come
from hands

Frozone's head is shaped
like a cold capsule

Lightning McQueen

Lightning McQueen was a hotshot rookie race car, poised to become the youngest car ever to win the Piston Cup Championship. At the start, he had just two things on his mind: winning and the perks that come with it. But that all changed after Lightning got lost in the forgotten town of Radiator Springs. There he was introduced to a group of new friends who changed his whole outlook on life.

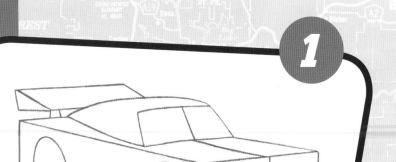

1

while he's competing in the races of the World Grand Prix, Lightning sports this tribute to Doc Hudson on his hood

2

for the World Grand Prix races, Lightning gets a new, sportier spoiler!

3

95

NITROADE
HI-ENERGY DRINK

PISTON RACING SERIES CUP

4

5

Mater

Mater is a friendly tow truck with a big heart, and he's always willing to lend a helping hook. He is the self-proclaimed world's best backward driver, who also gets a kick out of tractor tipping.

keep facial expressions off center to emphasize Mater's goofiness

YES!

YES!

NO!
too centered

1

2

YES!

mirrors are at irregular angles

NO!

mirrors are not perfectly aligned

3

4

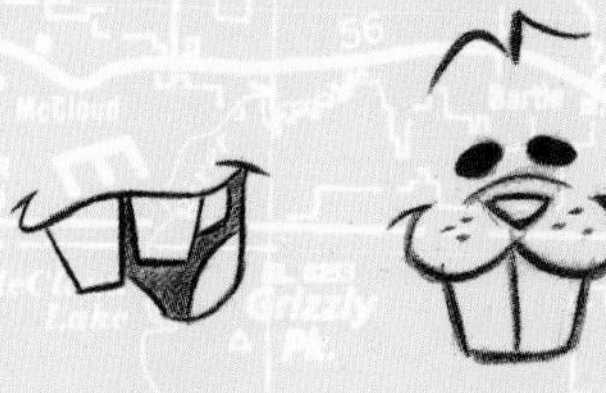

YES! ~~PORE~~ **NO!**

his misshapen buckteeth aren't perfect squares—and there's a gap between them

5

SPARKY'S SPARK PLUGS

Sally

Sally, a smart and beautiful sports car, is determined to restore Radiator Springs to the bustling town it was in its heyday. Originally an attorney from Los Angeles, she shows Lightning that sometimes it's good to live life in the slow lane.

1

Sally's eyebrows are heaviest at the peaks

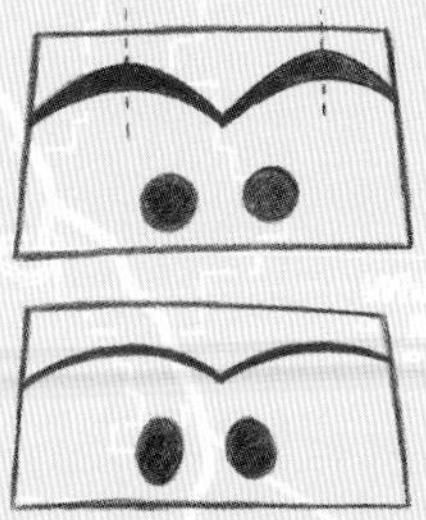

YES!

NO!

2

3

Sally is just about a tire-width smaller than Lightning

4

YES!
spokes
have
curved
pattern

NO!
not
straight

NO!
not
sharp

5

Doc Hudson

Doc is a respected and admired town doctor, and he's the judge in Radiator Springs. But he has a mysterious past. Protective of the town, Doc cherishes the quiet and simple life. At first, he wants nothing to do with the flashy race car Lightning McQueen, but he ends up becoming Lightning's mentor and friend.

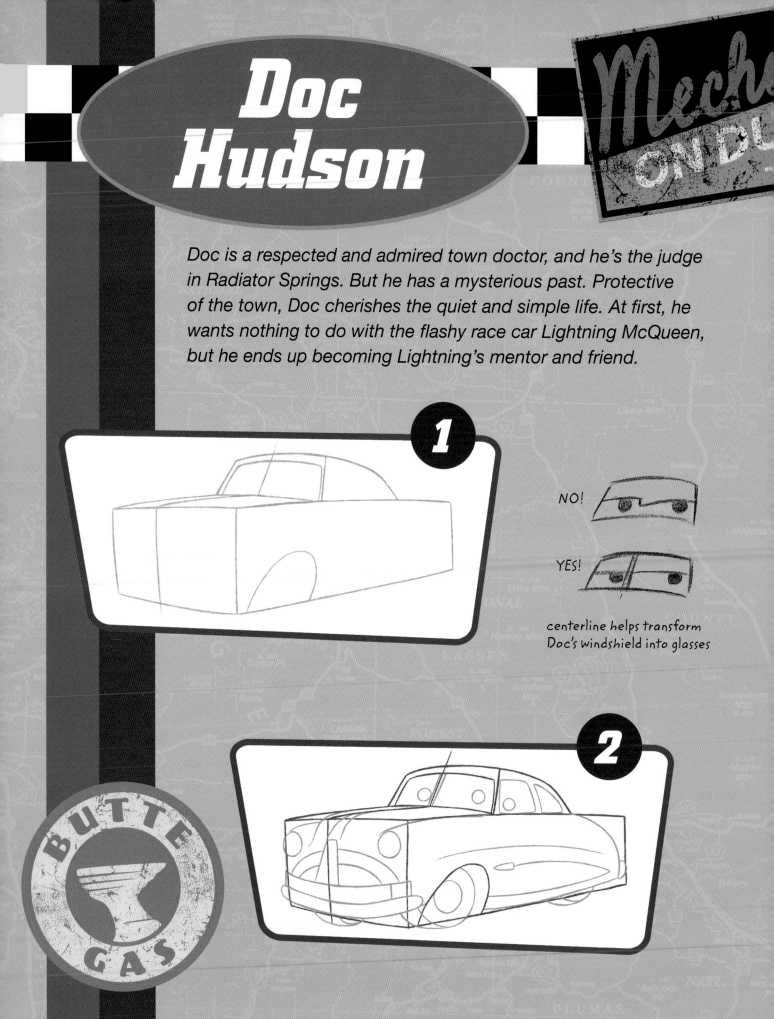

1

NO!

YES!

centerline helps transform
Doc's windshield into glasses

2

BUTTE GAS

3

Doc's grille is like a rainbow built over the central letter A

NO!
front fender
isn't round

YES!
fender curves
into front bumper

4

5

Carl Fredricksen

Carl Fredricksen is a shy 78-year-old who wishes people would leave him alone. Each morning Carl meticulously vacuums every surface and straightens every doily, making sure things are just as his beloved late wife, Ellie, left them. After his morning cleaning ritual, Carl eats the same breakfast he's eaten every day for the past 50 years. Then he puts on his hat, sits on his porch, and glares at people talking too loudly into their newfangled portable phones as they walk by.

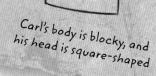

Carl's body is blocky, and his head is square-shaped

1

2

96

fingers are blocky

start with square glasses

cut in for nose

5

6

Carl is about 2 heads tall

Russell

Russell is Carl Fredricksen's neighbor. He has enough gear to make him the most prepared 8-year-old Junior Wilderness Explorer in Explorer history. The only problem is, he's never been anywhere except the Camping Museum downtown. Determined to get his "Assisting the Elderly" badge and be promoted to Senior Wilderness Explorer, Russell's dream is to attend the father-son ceremony so his dad can pin on Russell's new badge. First, Russell must hound Carl Fredricksen with assistance—even if it means following Carl to the ends of the globe and back.

body is roughly egg-shaped

1

2

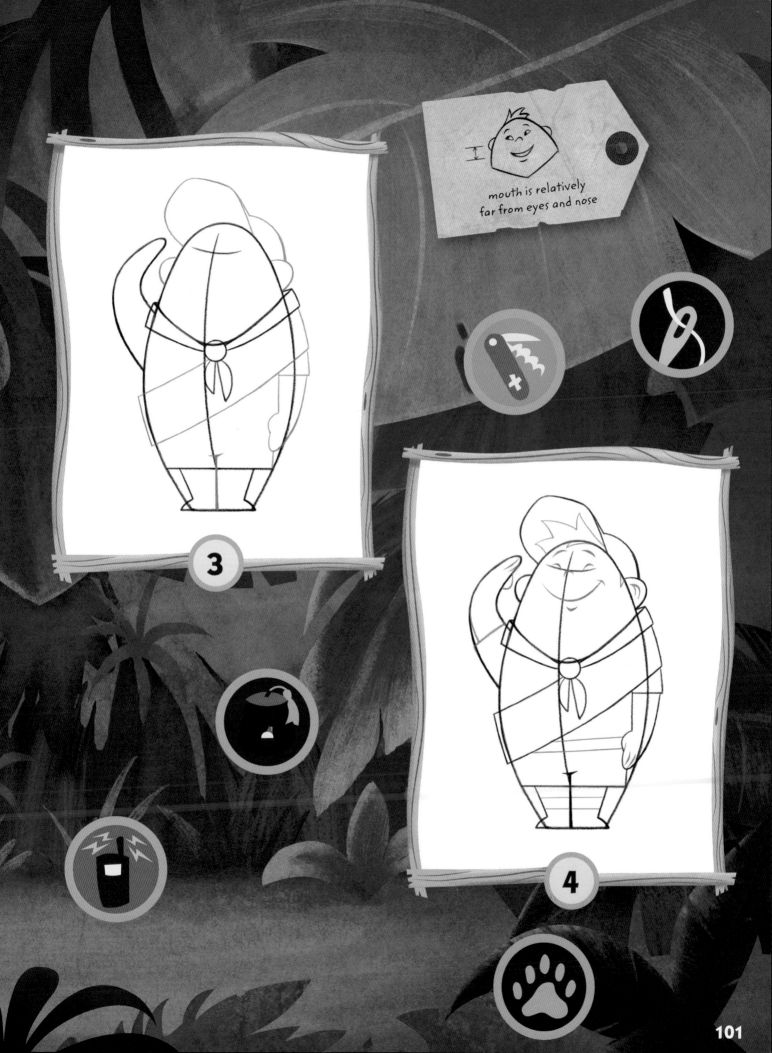

mouth is relatively
far from eyes and nose

3

4

start with simple flipper-like arms; then add fingers

5

6

Dug

Dug is a desperate dog who wants nothing more than to be part of a pack. Because of a technological invention, Dug can verbally communicate with humans. Unfortunately, this talking device doesn't help Dug much in the "brains" department, but he'll do anything to make his master happy. Dug must decide who deserves his loyalty—the pack he's known his entire life or this new pack with Carl and Russell.

nose swoops up

1

4

5

tail fur flares most in the middle

paws are small compared to body

6

7

WRECK-IT RALPH

Every day for 30 years, Wreck-It Ralph has worked as the Bad Guy in the arcade game *Fix-It Felix Jr.* But he's grown tired of smashing the Nicelanders' apartment building to bits, only to have the Good Guy, Fix-It Felix, repair it with his magic hammer and win a shiny gold medal. Ralph desperately wants to be the Good Guy for once.

1

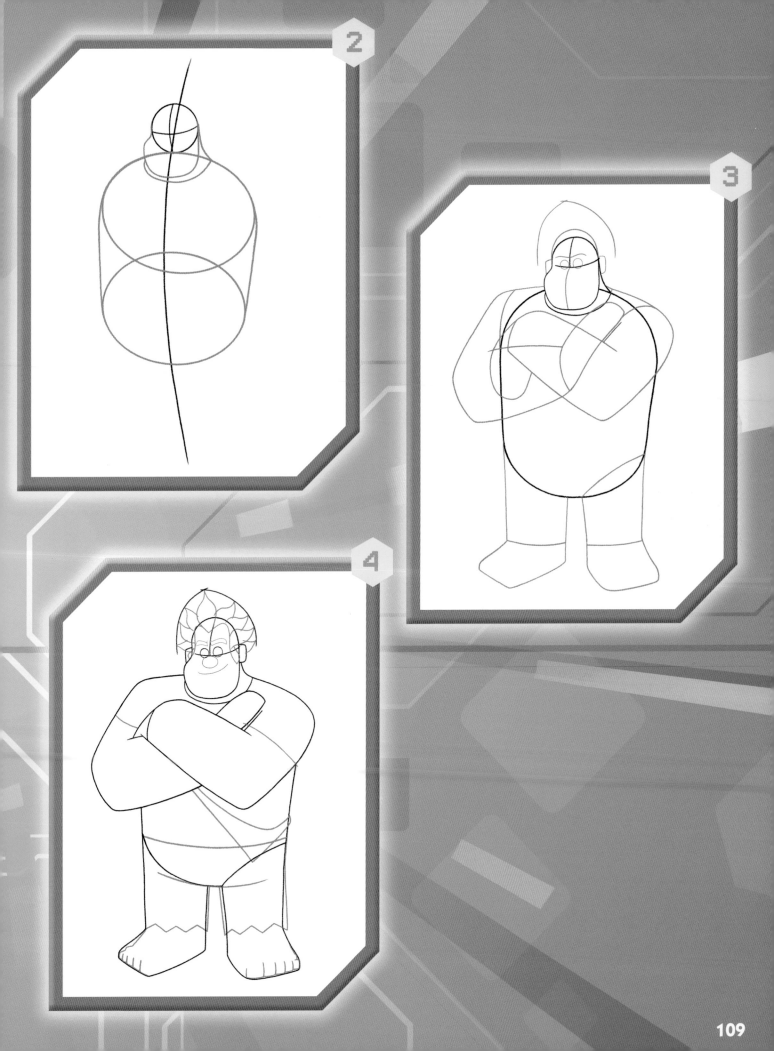

VANELLOPE

Vanellope von Schweetz is a programming mistake in the candy-coated kart-racing game *Sugar Rush*. All she wants is to be a racer, but King Candy, the ruler of *Sugar Rush*, has banned her from racing because she is a glitch. Vanellope meets Wreck-It Ralph when he stumbles into her game, and they team up to build a kart and train to win a race— and a whole lot more.

1

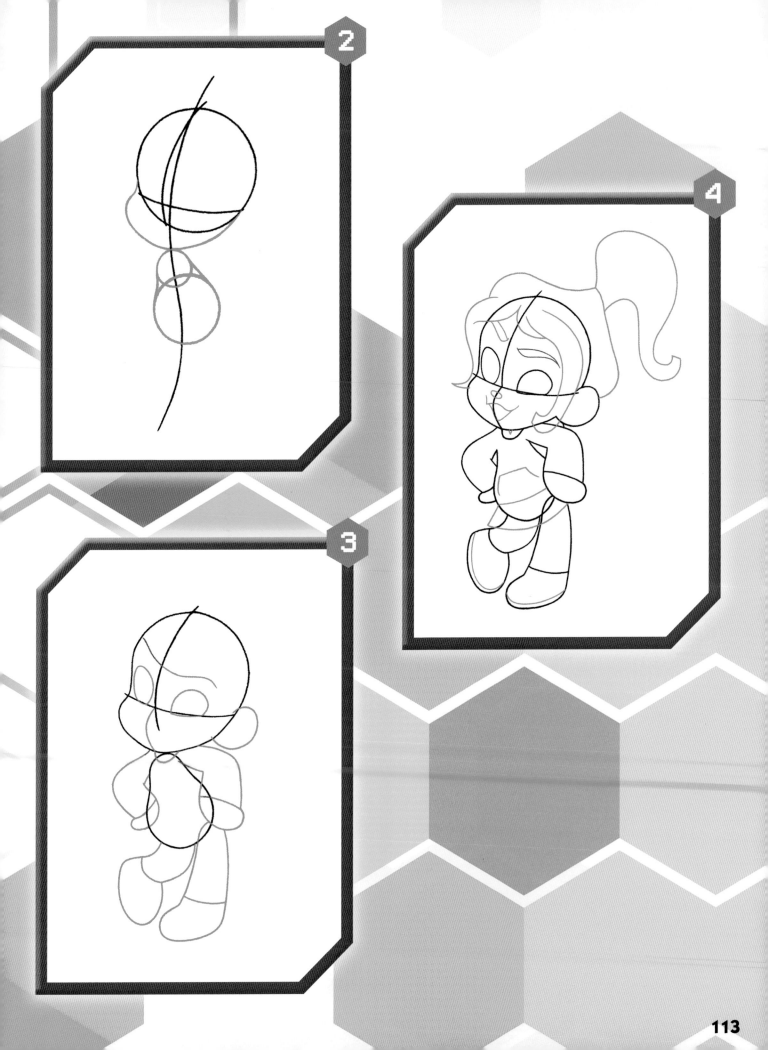

5

6

FIX-IT FELIX

It's nice being the Good Guy! In his arcade game, Fix-It Felix repairs the Nicelanders' apartment building every time Ralph wrecks it. Felix wields his magic hammer and yells, "I can fix it!" The Nicelanders give Felix a gold medal, while they hoist Ralph off the roof into a big mud puddle below.

1

2

![Disney PLANES]

DUSTY CROPHOPPER

Dusty is a plane with high hopes—literally. He sees himself soaring alongside his high-flying heroes in an international race. The fact that he's not really built for competitive racing doesn't stop him from pursuing his dream—but his fear of heights just might. With a little help from his friends, Dusty takes off on an adventure of a lifetime, daring to reach heights he never imagined possible.

decal behind Dusty's nose

①

②

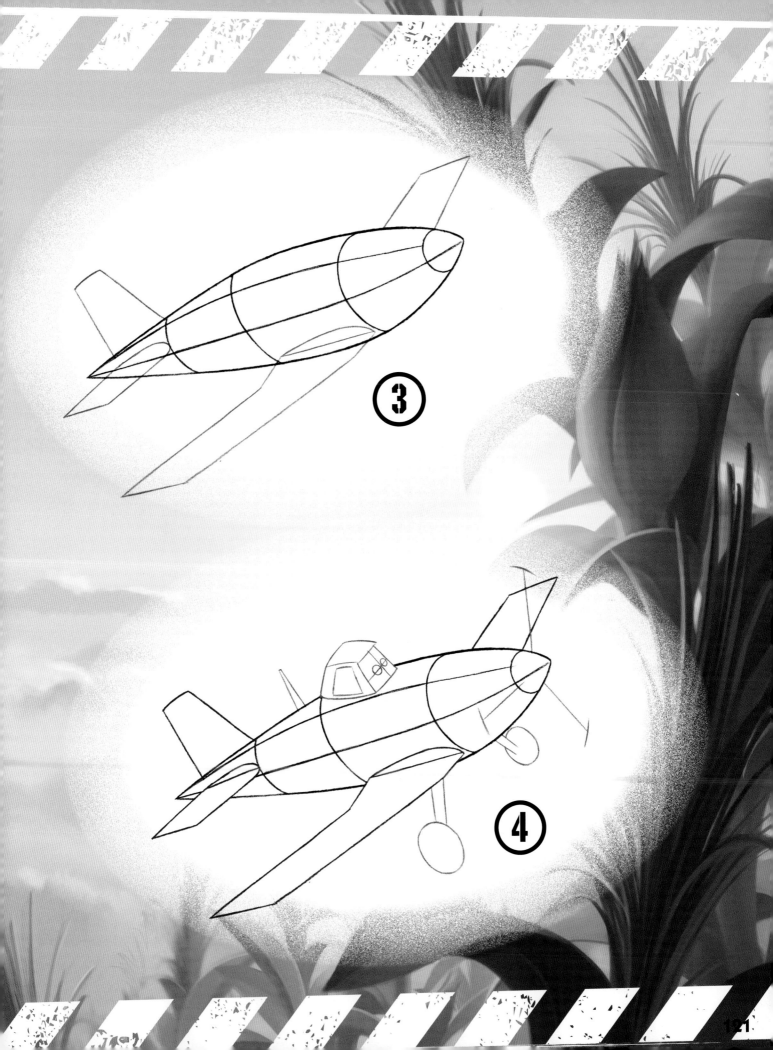

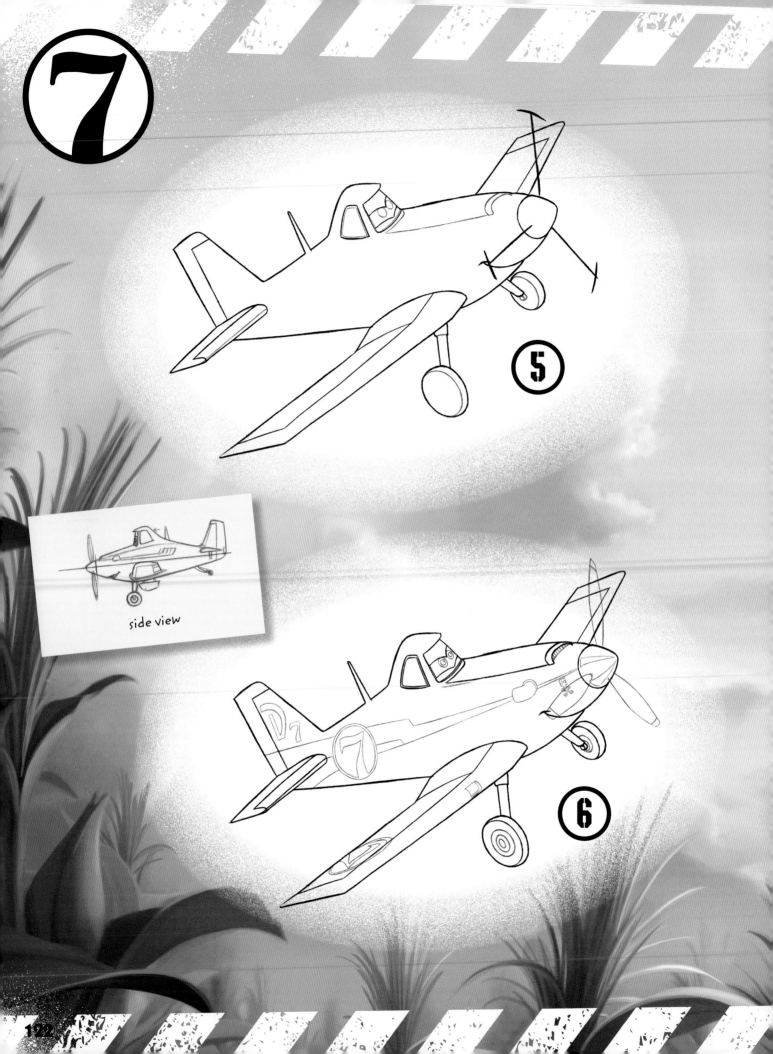

side view

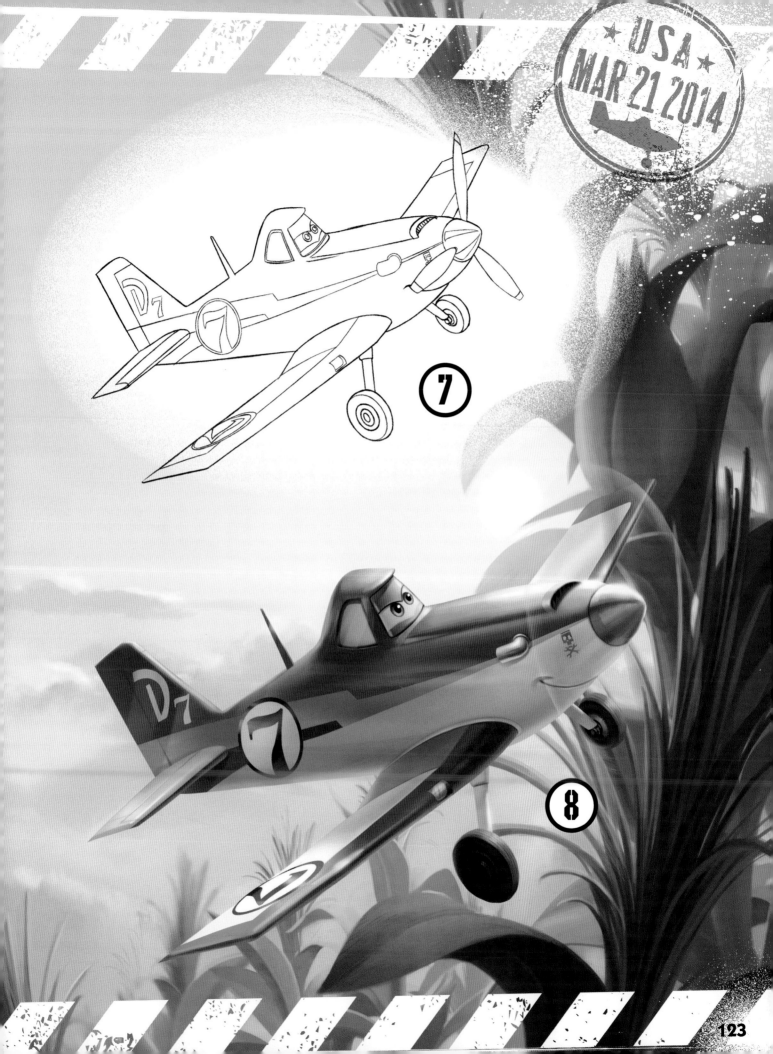

SKIPPER RILEY

A retired old Navy warplane, Skipper was an ace flier and top instructor of the esteemed Jolly Wrenches squadron until an incident during combat left him grounded for life. These days Skipper keeps to himself, but his quiet existence is turned upside-down when Dusty asks for his aerial expertise—and gets a few life lessons in the process. While coaching Dusty, Skipper finds that he also has a few things to learn.

①

②

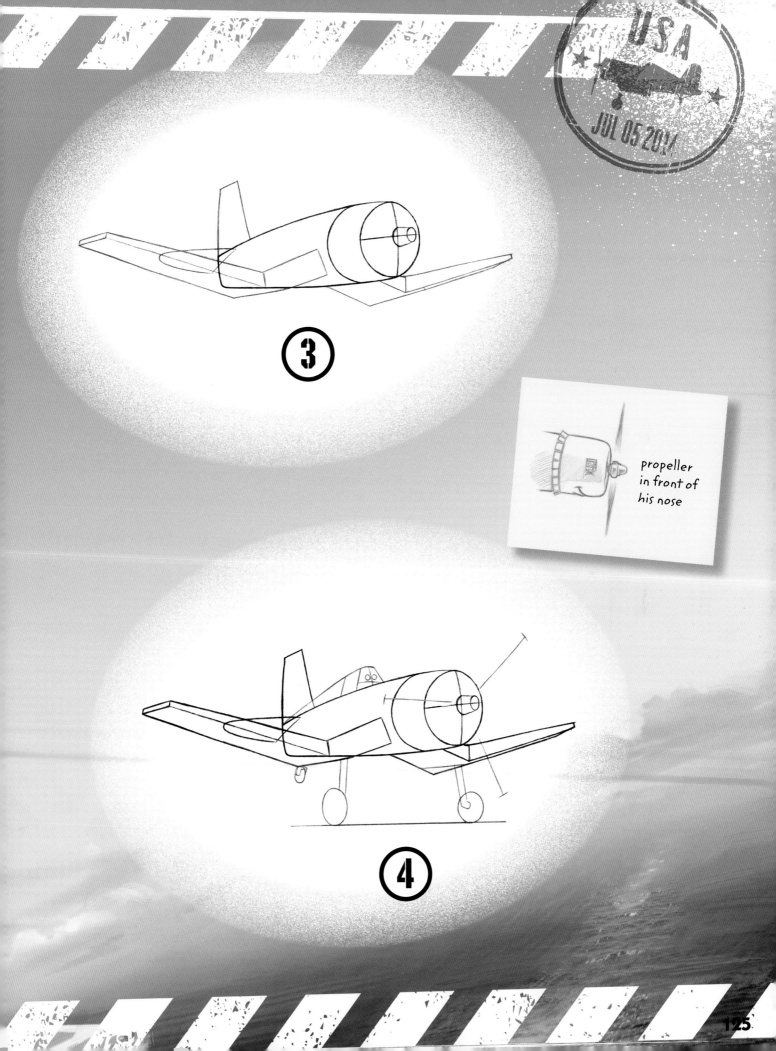

③

propeller
in front of
his nose

④

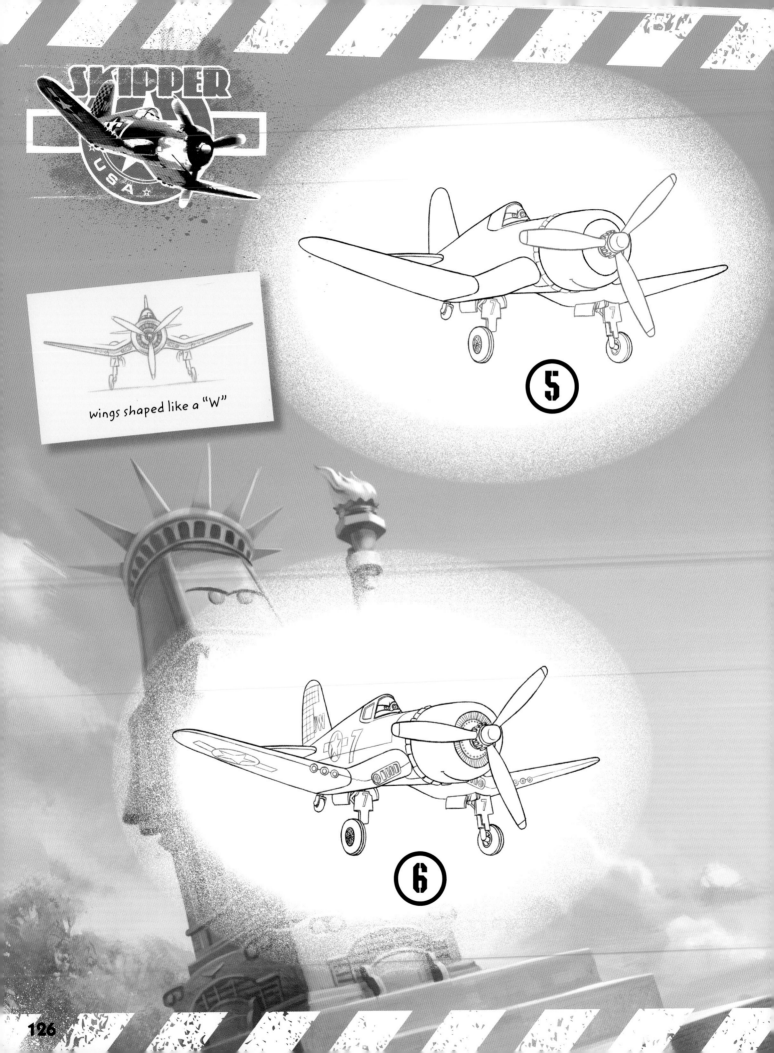

SKIPPER
USA

wings shaped like a "W"

⑤

⑥

⑦

Skipper's decal

⑧

EL CHUPACABRA

5

The extremely charming El Chupacabra is a legend in Mexico. (Just ask him!) Powered by his passion for racing, this champ is anything but low key—his booming voice and charismatic presence are as big as his oversized engine. No one really knows what is truth and what is delusion when it comes to El Chu, but one thing is beyond doubt: He races with a whole lot of heart and more dramatic flair than is recommended at high altitudes.

top view

①

②

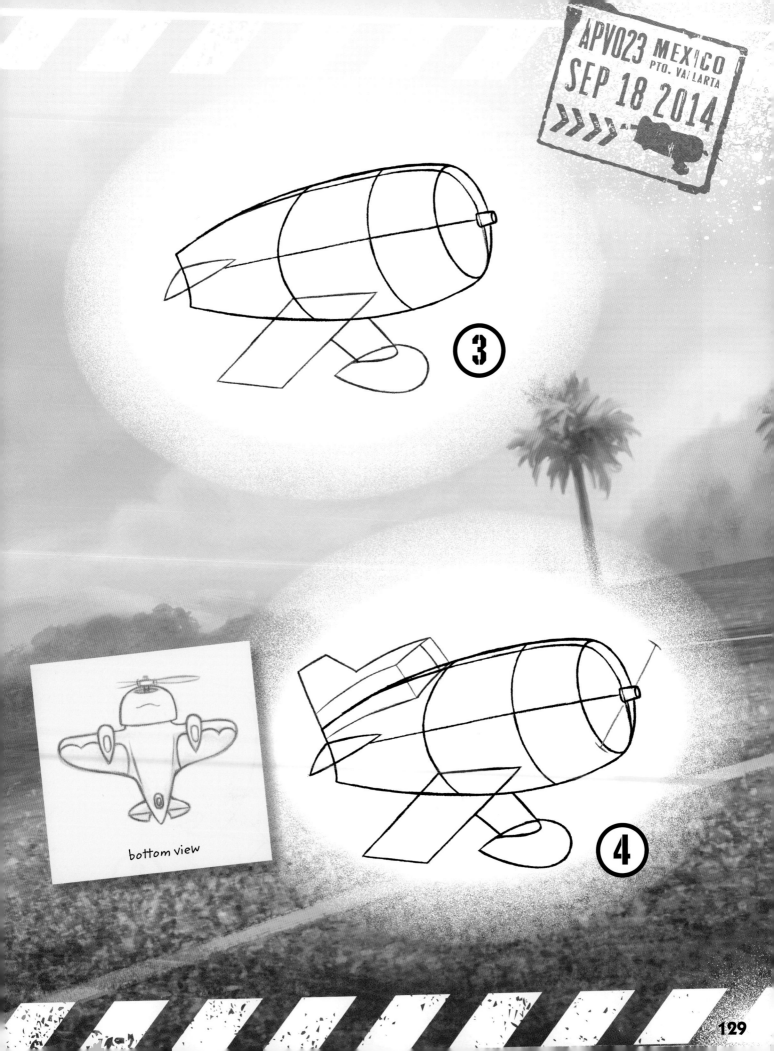

bottom view

③

④

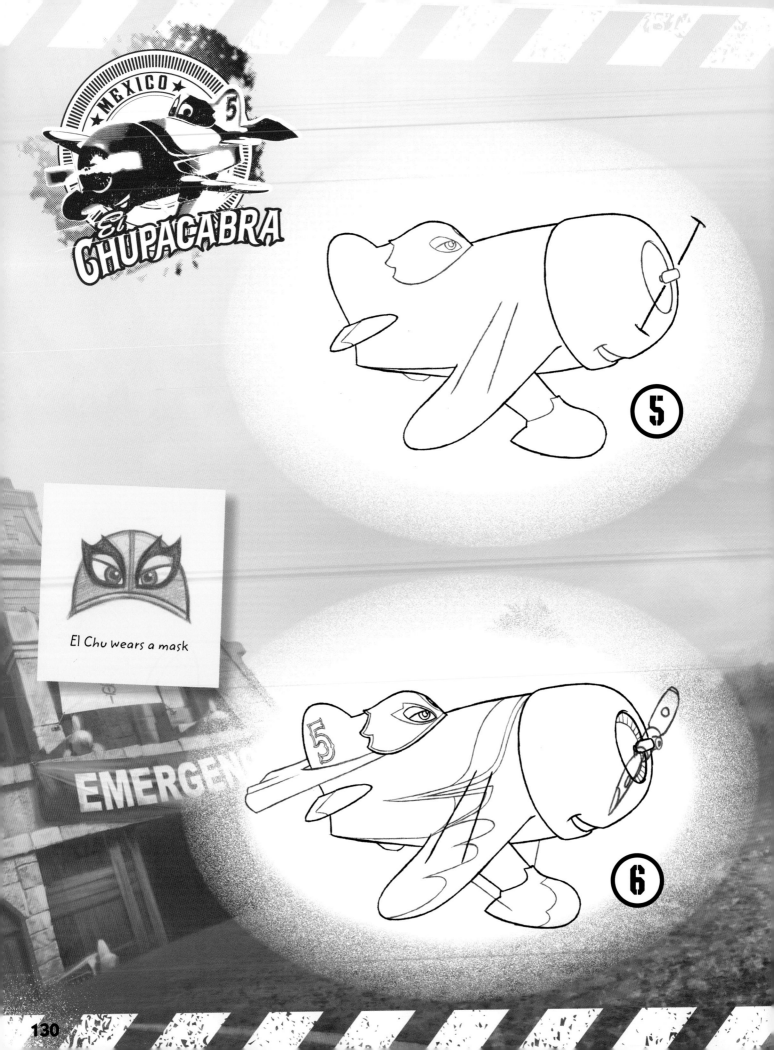

MEXICO ★ 5

El CHUPACABRA

El Chu wears a mask

⑤

⑥

5

⑦

5

decal shows he
is número cinco
(number 5)

⑧

MOANA

Moana is the 16-year-old daughter of Tui, the chief of Motuni. She is drawn to the ocean, beyond the safety of the reef. The open ocean is the only place the people of her village are forbidden to go. But when her island is threatened by a terrible darkness, Moana breaks the rules and sets sail on an epic adventure to save her world.

Moana's hands and feet are strong and rounded

NO! not thin and angular

3

4

5

Moana is about 5½ heads tall

6

7

almond-shaped eyes,
with thick eyelashes
and eyebrows

eyes are angled like this

MAUI

Maui is a demigod—half god, half mortal, all awesome. In his muscular and tattoo-covered arms, he wields his magical fishhook, using it to pull up whole islands from the sea. Charismatic and funny, he sets sail with Moana for the adventure of a lifetime.

Maui is 5 heads high

1   2   3   4

Maui's jaw consists of
4 lines crossing together

NO! not a single
rounded line

HEIHEI

Heihei is the village's resident rooster. The little rooster accidentally sets sail with Moana, joining her for an action-packed journey he was not prepared for.

4

5

Proportion Guide:

head line is ¼ from the top

neck line is halfway down

legs line is ¼ from the bottom

YES! eyes are looking in different directions

NO! not looking the same direction

Don't miss these other books by Walter Foster Jr.!

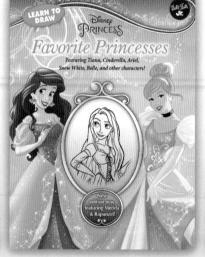

Learn to Draw Disney Villains

Draw the Disney characters you love to hate: Cruella De Vil, Maleficent, Captain Hook, the Queen of Hearts, Jafar, and more.

ISBN: 978-1-63322-678-4

Learn to Draw Disney Favorite Princesses

Learn to draw Snow White, Cinderella, Sleeping Beauty, Tiana, Ariel, Belle, Jasmine, Rapunzel, Merida, Mulan, and Pocahontas.

ISBN: 978-1-60058-145-8

Learn to Draw Disney Classic Animated Movies

Draw characters from *Alice in Wonderland, The Jungle Book, Peter Pan, Bambi, Pinocchio, Dumbo,* and *more.*

ISBN: 978-1-63322-135-2